MW00978247

Pacific Northwest Trail

Data Book

2018 Edition

Tim Youngbluth

Tim Youngbluth

Copyright © 2018 Tim Youngbluth
Youngbluth & Associates, LLC
All rights reserved.

ISBN-13: 978-1985314856
ISBN-10: 1985314851

This data book is written to compliment the
Pacific Northwest Trail Digest – 2018 Edition.

It is small and concise, designed to provide the thru-hiker or the section hiker with the vital mileage and landmark information needed while on the trail. It is an aid to a good set of trail maps.

The Pacific Northwest Trail (PNT) is one of the most challenging of the eleven national scenic trails. Always use good judgment while hiking, especially in the very remote areas of the PNT. There is no cell phone coverage for many areas of the PNT. Finding other hikers on the trail is considered a welcome, but rare, occurrence.

Comments and suggestions are most welcome. For a free loadable GPS file, in .gpx format, for all the landmarks listed in this book, contact the author at

3dtrails@gmail.com.

Front Cover: PNT trailhead sign at Lake Ann Trail 600 crossing the Swift Creek Trail 607
48° 50.022'N 121° 39.449'W 4120'

Courtesy of Ashley Hill, PNT 2016 Thru-Hiker

PERMITS and RESERVATIONS

Backcountry permits and campsite reservations are required for only three areas of the trail.

Glacier National Park

There is a $40 charge for advance applications in addition to a $7 per person/per night camping fee. Applications should be sent to:

> Backcountry Reservations
> Glacier National Park
> West Glacier, MT 59936
> 406-888-5819 (fax)

Walk-up permits and camp site reservations are also available; nearly half of all the backcountry campgrounds are held for walk-ins, but those with reservations have a better chance of obtaining their desired campsites. Permits may be obtained at Apgar and St. Mary's Visitor Centers, and the Many Glacier, Two Medicine, and Polebridge ranger stations. Fees apply to walk-up services also.

Ross Lake National Recreation Area and North Cascades National Park

One Wilderness Information Center supports the North Cascades National Park, and the Ross Lake and Lake Chelan National Recreation Areas. A permit is required for all backcountry travel in these areas. There are no backcountry permits reservations. Their phone number is (360) 854-7245 and they closed during the winter.

Olympic National Park

Wilderness Camping Permits are required for all overnight stays in Olympic National Park wilderness (backcountry) and reservations are need for some camp sites as noted in this book. Call the Wilderness Information Center (WIC) to check on station hours and seasonal equipment and permit requirements.

The WIC is co-located at the

> Olympic National Park Visitor Center
> 3002 Mount Angeles Road,
> Port Angeles, WA 98362.
> (360) 565-3100.

The fee for each wilderness camping permit is $8 per person per night or $45 for an annual pass. There is no nightly charge for youth 15 years of age and under but they still count towards the group size. Wilderness fees are non-refundable.

RESUPPLY OPTIONS

31.5 Waterton, Canada: (6.1 mi north via ferry). $32 one-way, $49 round trip. US or Canadian passport required. No other passports are accepted. *No*

55.2 Polebridge: On the primary route. No post office. *Hostel*

133.6 Eureka: This is the center of town along the primary PNT route. Post Office: 113 14th St, Eureka, MT 59917 (406) 297-2132 *yes*

190.8 Yaak: The town is 7.3 miles south following Road 508. No post office. *No → ride to train in Libby*

261.1 Bonners Ferry: South on US95 for about 15 miles. Post Office: 7167 1st Street, Bonners Ferry, ID 83805. (208) 267-3302

347.1 Metaline Falls: One of the best trail towns on the PNT! Post office: 224 E 5th Ave, Metaline Falls, WA 99153 (509) 446-2425

389.3 Northport: Another good trail town right on the primary route. Post Office: 409 Center Ave, Northport, WA 99157 509-732-6660

420.2 Orient: This is as small hamlet 3.7 miles south on US395. Dangerous road shoulder. Small general store. Post Office: 365 Main St., Orient, WA 99160 (509) 684-5886

477.1, 495.9, 518.8 Republic: There are three waypoints that offer paved road access to this great trail town. Post Office: 128 N Clark St., Republic, WA 99166-9998   509-775-3332

578.5 Oroville: This is the half way point on the PNT with exceptional opportunities to resupply before heading into the Pasayten wilderness for a week or longer. Post office: 1234 Ironwood St, Oroville, WA 98844 (509) 476-2393

604.3 Loomis: Loomis is a small village 2 miles south of PNT. Post Office: 12 Palmer Ave. Loomis, WA 98827   509-223-4351 (Limited hours). Convenience store is closed.

736.9 Ross Lake Resort: The resort <u>may not</u> offer mail drop services in 2018. In 2016 the provided the service with a $20 pickup fee (cash). Since the staff only picks up mail about once a week and drives nearly 100 mile round-trip to get it, it is best to plan ahead. It is best to call them in advance to check.   Their phone number is 206.386.4437 (May-November). There is no store for resupply at the resort.

799.5 Glacier: About 13 miles west on the Mount Baker Highway. No post office.

841.1 Concrete: The town is about 11 miles south; first going 7 miles on the Baker Lake Road, and then turning on Burpee Hill Road to State Route 20. Post Office: 45650 Main St., Concrete, WA 98237   360-853-8311

913.0 Alger, WA - Convenience Store 0.7 mi south of PNT on Old Highway 99N. Or, a convenience store and bus stop 0.9 miles west at I-5. No post office.

951.8 Anacortes: Directly on the PNT primary route, most of the stores and restaurants can be found on the north-south Commercial Avenue/SR20.   Post Office: 519 Commercial Ave., Anacortes, WA 98221 360-299-6689

976.4 Oak Harbor: This town provides multiple places for resupply and lodging along the two mile stretch of SR20 south of the waypoint. Post Office: 32199 WA-20, Oak Harbor, WA 98277 (360) 675-3000.

993.4 Coupeville: Hike about 2.4 miles north on Ebey's Landing Road to reach this small, quiet farming, waterfront community. Post Office: 201 NW Coveland St., Coupeville, WA 98239 360-678-5353

1000.4 Port Townsend: The grocery store is one mile south of the ferry dock on SR20, one block west of the trail. Post Office: 1332 Washington St. Port Townsend, WA 98368 360-379-2996.

1108.8 Port Angeles: Follow Olympic Hot Springs Road 4 miles north to US101, then 3 miles east on to find a small mini mart. The nearest grocery store is Albertsons in Port Angeles, about 8 miles east on US101. Post Office: 424 E. 1st St., Port Angeles, WA 98362 360-417-7528.

1162.0 Forks: The town is about 6 miles west and north on U.S. Highway 101. Post Office: 61 S, Spartan Ave. Forks, WA 98331 360-374-6303. *Pick up bear cannister*

1196.6 La Push: On the PNT entering town; Lonesome Creek General Store & Post Office: 500 Ocean Dr., La Push, WA 98350 360-374-5378 (Limited hours)

IDAHO

Total Mileage	Dist.	Elev.	Fac.	Landmark
219.7	0.3	6000'	TX	Trail 42 X Ruby Ridge Trail 35
221.6 *huckleberries!	1.9	5880'	Rd-C	Trail 35 X Copper Ridge Road 403 and Trail Camp (no water)
225.5	3.9	4740'	Rd	Trail 35 X Forest Road 2517
225.6	0.1	4790'	W	Spring (0.1 mi southeast on FR2517)
227.9	2.3	2980	TX	Trail 35 X Trail 205
229.6	1.7	2580'	C	Trail Camp
231.2	1.6	2750'	TX-C-W	Forest Road 2202 X Bussard Mountain Trail 32 and Trail Camp
235.5	4.3	5710'	TX	Trail 32 X Old Jeep Trail
236.0	0.5	5930'	TX	Trail 32 X Danquist Trail 225
238.4	2.4	5300'	TX	Trail 225 X Trail 23
240.0	1.6	4200'	W	Rock Creek (water?)
240.7	0.7	3840'	Rd	Trail 23 X Camp Nine Mile Road 397
240.9	0.2	3830'	W	Rock Creek
242.2	1.3	3490'	BW	Dry Bushwhack West (alternate)
242.5	0.3	3470'	Rd	Road 397 @ Brush Lake Bushwhack
243.6	1.1	3030'	BW	Bushwhack @ Brush Lake Creek
244.4	0.8	3010'	Rd	Bushwhack X Forest Road 1004 @ Brush Lake

Total Mileage	Dist.	Elev.	Fac.	Landmark
244.8	*0.4*	*3010'*	*C*	*Brush Lake Camp (0.4 south of PNT)*
246.1	1.7	2500'	Rd	Forest Road 1004 X Camp 9 Road – Old US Highway 95
261.1	*15.0*	*1870'*	*R*	*Bonners Ferry, Idaho (15 mi south of PNT)*
254.9	8.8	1850'	Rd	Kerr Lake Road-45C X West Side Road 18
255.1	0.2	1900'	TH-C	West Side Rd X Trail 14 / Parker Ridge Trail 221 - Parker Creek Trail Camp (Must Fill Water!)
261.9	6.8	5940'	C	Trail 221 @ Parker Ridge Trail Camp (no water)
262.9	1.0	6290'	C	Trail Camp (no water)
264.2	1.3	6680'	C	Trail Camp (no water)
265.2	1.0	7060'	TX	Trail 221 X Parker Peak Summit Trail (Dry campsite)
265.7	0.5	6860'	TX	Trail 221 X Parker Lake Trail 203
266.3	*0.6*	*6330'*	*C*	*Parker Lake Trail Camp (0.6 mi north of PNT-- steep descent/climb)*
269.2	3.5	7110'	TX	Trail 221 X Long Mountain Lake Trail 15
269.7	*0.5*	*6730'*	*C*	*Long Mountain Lake Trail Camp (0.4 mi northeast of PNT -steep descent/climb)*
270.1	0.9	6400'	TX	Trail 221 X Pyramid Pass Trail 13
271.2	1.1	5820'	TX	Trail 13 X Ball Lakes Trail 43 (signed)
271.6	0.4	6070'	C	Pyramid Lake Trail Camp

Total Mileage	Dist.	Elev.	Fac.	Landmark
272.5	0.9	6730'	C	Ball Lake Trail Camp #1
273.0	0.5	6630'	C-BW	Trail 43 @ Ball Lakes Trail camp #2 and Bushwhack Start
273.9	0.9	6780'		Turn Point West on Bushwhack
278.0	4.1	4370'	TX	Bushwhack X Lion Creek Trail 42 (est.)
278.7	0.7	4110'	C	Trail Camp @ Kent Creek X Lion Creek
279.6	0.9	3860	C	Trail Camp at natural water slide
279.9	0.3	3720'	Rd	Trail 42 X Lion Creek Road – RD42
281.8	1.9	3210'	Rd	Forest Road 42 X Forest Road 423
284.0	2.2	4600'	W	Creek (Last reliable water)
286.5	2.5	6480'		Trail 37 below Lookout Mountain summit
287.6	1.1	5510'	TX/Rd	Trail 37 X Lookout Lake Trail 36 X Lucky Creek Road (Dry Trail Camp)
288.2	0.6	5350'	TX	Lucky Creek Road X Trail 37
291.6	3.4	3410'	Rd	Trail 37 X Lucky Creek Road 43
293.7	2.1	2580'	Rd	Road 43 X East Shore Road RD1
294.6	0.9	2480'	TH	East Shore Road RD1 X Floss Creek Trail 42
295.2	*0.6*	*2460'*	*C*	*Idaho State Lionhead Campground (0.6 miles south of PNT - Fee)*
304.6	*10.0*	*2480'*	*C*	*Idaho State Indian Creek Campground (10 mi south of PNT - limited supplies)*
296.2	1.6	2520'	TX	Trail 42 X Spur Trail to Geisinger Camp

Total Mileage	Dist.	Elev.	Fac.	Landmark
296.5	*0.3*	*2450'*	*C*	*Geisinger Camp (0.3 mi west of PNT)*
297.1	0.9	2760'	TX	Trail 42 X Upper Priest Lake Trail 302
298.1	1.0	2450'	C	Lakeshore Trail Camp
299.4	1.3	2450'	C	Trail 302 @ Upper Priest Lk Trapper Camp
303.5	4.1	2640'	Rd-C	Trail 302 X Forest Road 655 and Trail Camp
303.9	0.4	2630'	Rd	Forest Road 655 X Forest Road 1013
308.2	4.3	2770'	TH	Forest Road 1014 X Upper Priest River Trail 308
308.9	0.7	2770'	TX	Trail 308 X Trail 317
310.2	1.3	3540'	Rd	Trail 317 X Forest Road 1134
315.2	5.0	5010'		Trail 315 @ End of Switchbacks
316.6	1.4	5390'		Trail 315 'Y' Split
317.7	1.1	5940'	TX	Trail 315 X Shedroof Divide Trail 512

WASHINGTON

Total Mileage	Dist.	Elev.	Fac.	Landmark
320.1	2.4	6300'	TX	Trail 512 X Salmo-Divide Trail 535 and Trail Camp
322.3	2.2	5500'	TX	Trail 512 X Shedroof Cutoff Trail 511 (estimated)
324.0	1.7	4340'	Rd	Trail 511 X Forest Road 2220
324.9	0.9	4360'	W	Deermer Creek

Total Mileage	Dist.	Elev.	Fac.	Landmark
326.7	1.8	4720'	W	Leola Creek
329.2	2.5	5560'	TH	Road 260 X Crowell Ridge Trail 515
332.9	3.7	6630	TX	Trail 515 X North Fork Trail 507
335.6	2.7	4560	TX	Trail 507 X Slate Creek Trail 525
336.1	0.5	3990'	C	Trail Camp
337.8	1.7	3720	TX	Trail 507 X Red Bluff Trail 553
338.3	0.5	3620'	TX	Trail 507 X Halliday Trail 522
343.1	4.8	2580'	Rd	Trail 507 X Lime Lake Road
347.1	4.0	2090'	R	State Route 31 @ Metaline Falls, Washington
348.2	1.1	2150'	Rd	State Route 31 X Boundary Road
351.8	3.6	2580'	Rd	Boundary Road X Flume Creek Road – RD350
353.7	1.9	3230'		Flume Creek
359.0	5.3	5130'	TH	Forest Road 350 X Flume Creek Trail 502
362.6	3.6	7130'	TX	Trail 502 X Abercrombie Mountain Trail 117
364.6	2.0	5820'	TX	Trail 117 X North Fork Silver Creek Trail 119
370.3	5.7	3130'	Rd	Trail 119 X Silver Creek Road – RD070 and NFS Camp
373.9	3.6	2130'	Rd	Forest Road 70 X Deep Lake Boundary Road – RD9445
376.7	2.8	2590'	W	O'Hare Creek
380.1	3.4	4340'	C	O'Hare Creek Road X Lind Ranch and Trail Camp

Total Mileage	Dist.	Elev.	Fac.	Landmark
384.2	4.1	1860'	Rd	Black Canyon Road X Aladdin Road – RD700
389.3	5.1	1360'	R	State Route 25 @ Northport, Washington Post Office: 409 Center Ave, Northport, WA 99157 509-732-6660
394.6	5.3	1930'	C - F	Sheep Creek Road @ Washington State Campground. $5
395.9	1.3	2030'	TH	Sheep Creek Road X Forest Road 15
401.8	5.9	2620'	Rd	Forest Road 4220 X Forest Road 670 / 290
402.9	1.1	2880'	Rd	Forest Road 15 X Forest Road 600
403.2	*0.3*	*2900'*	*C*	***NFS Elbow Lake Camp (no fee - 0.3 mi southeast of PNT)***
404.5	1.6	3290'	C	Trail Camp at Spring
404.6	0.1	3310'	Rd	Forest Road 15 X Forest Road 170
405.9	1.3	3170'	Rd	Forest Road 170 X Churchill Mine Road – RD1520
412.4	6.5	2150'	Rd	Forest Road 1520 X Sand Creek Road – RD4013
413.8	*1.4*	*2060'*	*C-F*	***NFS Pierre Lake Camp (Fee - 1.4 mi south of PNT) $6***
416.3	3.9	1470'	Rd	Sand Creek Road – RD4013 X Rock Cut Road - RD4141
416.4	0.1	1410'	W	Kettle River (private property)
416.5	0.1	1510'	Rd	Forest Road 4013 X Highway US 395

Total Mileage	Dist.	Elev.	Fac.	Landmark
420.2	*3.7*	*1440'*	**R**	*Town of Orient (3.7 mi south of PNT). Post Office: 365 Main St , Orient, WA 99160 (509) 684-5886*
420.3	3.8	2800'	Rd	Forest Road 595 X Forest Road 9576
423.7	3.4	4170'	Rd	Forest Road 9576 X Forest Road 300
425.8	2.1	4920'	Rd-C	Forest Road 300 X Forest Road 340 X Forest Road 450 and Trail Camp
427.9	2.1	5540'	Rd	Forest Road 400 X Forest Road 420 / 430
429.9	2.0	4860'	TX-C	Forest Road 400 X Forest Road 488 and Trail Camp
430.1	*0.2*	*4910'*	*W*	*Tiny - Noonday Spring (0.15 mi north of PNT)*
431.0	1.1	4330'	TX-C	Forest Road 450 X Forest Road 215 and great Trail Camp
433.5	2.5	4500'	TH C-F	Boulder Creek Road X Kettle Crest Trail 13 and Boulder Creek Summit Camp
436.7	3.2	5430'	TX	Trail 13 X Taylor Ridge Road – RD430
437.3	0.6	5140'	W	Creek - Good Water
442.4	5.1	5180'	TX	Trail 13 X Big Lick Trail 30
443.5	1.1	5510'	TX	Trail 13 X Mount Leona Loop Trail 49a
444.2	0.7	5510'	TX	Trail 13 X Stickpin Trail 71
446.4	2.2	6180'	C	Neff Spring - Trail Camp
447.8	1.4	6130'	W	Midnight Spring

Total Mileage	Dist.	Elev.	Fac.	Landmark
448.5	0.7	6070'	TH	Trail 13 X Old Stage Road Trails 1 / 75
449.7	1.2	7140'		Trail 13 @ Copper Butte Summit
452.7	3.0	6870'	TX	Trail 13 X Wapaloosie Mountain Trail 15
454.0	1.3	6540'	C	Piped Spring - Trail Camp
457.9	3.9	6130'	TX	Trail 13 X Columbia Mountain Trail 24 and Spring (light flow)
459.8	1.9	5460'	C	New NFS Horse Camp (no water)
460.1	0.3	5440'	Rd	Trail 13 X State Route 20 @ Sherman Pass
477.1	*17.0*	*2570'*	*R*	*Republic (17 mi west of PNT). Post Office: 128 N Clark St.., Republic, WA 99166-9998 509-775-3332*
460.7	0.6	5830'	W	Creek - Good Flow
462.4	1.7	6450'	W	Tiny Stream - wet trail
463.6	1.2	6330'	TX	Trail 13 X Snow Peak Trail 10
465.8	2.2	5980'	TX	Trail 13 X Edds Mountain Trail 3
467.5	1.7	6100'	BW	Trail 3 @ Bushwhack Point
470.0	2.5	4650'	BW	Bushwhack @ Hall Creek Ponds
470.4	0.4	4590'	Rd	Bushwhack X Hall Creek Road - Forest Road 600
472.0	1.6	4330'	TH	Forest Road 600 X Thirteen Mile Trail 23
476.1	4.1	4430'	TX	Trail 23 X Bear Pot Trail 19
476.8	*0.7*	*4180*	*W*	*Bear Pot Pond - stagnant / Shelberg Cabin crushed*

Total Mileage	Dist.	Elev.	Fac.	Landmark
478.6	2.5	4520'	Rd	Trail 23 X Forest Road 300
481.3	2.7	3560'	Rd	Trail 23 X Thirteenmile Road – RD2054
481.4	0.2	3690'	BW	Trail 23 X Bushwhack Point.
482.3	0.9	4040'	BW	Bushwhack @ Cougar Mountain
484.0	1.7	3480'	BW	Bushwhack @ Dry Run Pond
485.7	1.7	2110'	BW	Bushwhack X State Route 21
486.4	0.7	2170'	C	State Route 21 X Ten Mile Trail 25 and NFS Camp
495.9	*9.5*	*2570'*	*R*	*Republic (9.5 mi north of PNT). Post Office: 128 N Clark St.., Republic, WA 99166-9998 509-775-3332*
488.6	2.2	3360'	Rd	Trail 25 X Forest Road 100
490.4	1.8	3110'	Rd	Bushwhack X Scatter Creek Road – RD53
490.7	0.3	3430'	Rd	Bushwhack X Ferry Lake Campground Road – RD100
492.1	1.4	3710'	Rd	Bushwhack X Swan Lake Campground – Forest Road 500
493.5	1.4	3880'	Rd	Bushwhack X Unnamed Forest Road
494.0	0.5	3770'	Rd	Forest Road 5314 X Forest Road 500
495.0	1.0	3860	C	Trail Camp - no water
495.4	0.4	3890'	C-W	Grassy trail camp next to spring

Total Mileage	Dist.	Elev.	Fac.	Landmark
496.8	1.4	3750'	Rd	Forest Road 020 X Forest Road 030
498.2	1.4	3660'	FR	Forest Road 020 X Forest Road 3120
498.7	0.5	3820'	W	Ogle Creek - Water ?
503.5	4.8	4150'	Rd	Forest Road 200 X Forest Road 3125
504.7	1.2	4190'	Rd	Forest Road 3125 X Forest Road 31
509.6	4.9	3460'	W	Forest Road 31 @ Granite Creek
510.1	0.5	3520'	Rd-C	Forest Road 31 X State Route 20 and Stealth Trail Camp
518.8	**8.7**	*2570'*	***R***	***Republic (8.7 mi east of PNT). Post Office: 128 N Clark St.., Republic, WA 99166-9998 509-775-3332***
512.9	2.8	4880	TX	Trail 301 X Trail 310A
514.2	1.3	5030'	W	Hunter Spring
515.5	1.3	5170'	TX-W	Trail 301 X Clackamas Mountain Trail 302 and Pass Spring
518.6	3.1	3510'	Rd	Trail 301 X Cougar Creek Road – RD3510-100
520.5	1.9	3110'	W	Cougar Creek Access
521.3	0.8	2960'	Rd	Forest Road X County Road 5495
524.7	3.4	3570'	Rd	Road 5495 X Bunch Road – RD 4975
527.2	2.5	4110'	Rd	Road 4975 X Forest Road (Trail) RD 030
530.4	3.2	3570'	Rd	Forest Road 010 X Bonaparte Lake Road – RD 32

Total Mileage	Dist.	Elev.	Fac.	Landmark
531.0	*0.6*	*3570'*	*R?*	***Bonaparte Lake Resort (0.6 mi north of PNT - mail drop?) 615 Bonaparte Lake Road, Tonasket Washington, 98855; 509-486-2828***
530.9	0.5	3570'	TH-CF	NFS Bonaparte Lake Campground @ Pipsissewa Trail 383
531.7	0.8	4030'	W	Spring (PVC pipe - approx. location)
533.0	1.3	4420'	C	Trail Camp (no water)
533.5	0.5	4560'	TH	Forest Road 100 X South Side Trail 308
534.1	0.6	5060'	W	Duff Spring - Wet Trail
535.6	1.5	5780'	W	Creek - Wood Bridge
535.8	0.2	5830'	TX	Trail 308 X Fourth of July Trail 307
537.9	2.1	6030'	W	Lightning Spring
540.3	2.4	5710'	TX	Trail 307 @ Southern Most Point
542.5	2.2	5120'	W	Trail 307 X Spur Trail to Trailhead
544.5	2.0	4890'	W	Antoine Creek West
544.6	0.1	4880'	TX	Trail 307 X Antoine Trail 304
545.5	0.9	4410'	Rd	Trail 304 X Forest Road 150
547.9	2.4	3910'	Rd	Forest Road 100 X Mill Creek Road – RD 3230
548.2	*0.3*	*3540'*	*W*	***Church Spigot (0.3 mi north of PNT)***
550.0	2.1	3460'	Rd	Road 9467 X Swanson Creek Road – RD 4662

Tim Youngbluth

Total Mileage	Dist.	Elev.	Fac.	Landmark
555.8	5.8	3410'	W	Road 4759 X Mount Wilcox Road – RD 3524-100
561.0	5.2	3770'	Rd	"Mount Wilcox Road" X Summit Lake Road – RD 3525
561.2	0.2	3710'	W	Twin Springs ("stock water")
563.6	2.4	4230'	Rd	Road 3525 X Forest Road 100 - Whistler Canyon Trail
564.6	*1.0*	*4270'*	*C*	*DNR Summit Lake Camp (1.0 mi north of PNT); reported disgusting.*
568.6	5.0	3180'	C	Whistler Canyon Trail @ Bluff Camp (No water)
571.2	2.6	2920'	W	Whistler Canyon Trail @ Spring (est. - water ?)
573.3	2.1	2200'	W	Whistler Canyon Creek
575.7	2.4	950'	Rd	Whistler Canyon Trail X US Highway 97
578.5	2.8	940'	R-TH	Similkaneen Trail @ Oroville Post office: 1234 Ironwood St, Oroville, WA 98844 (509) 476-2393
579.8	*1.3*	*920'*	*C-Fr*	*Osoyoos Lake Veteran's Memorial Park (1.3 mi north of PNT). $16, reservation reg'd.*
580.0	1.5	1040'	TH	Similkaneen Trail X Loomis-Oroville Road

Total Mileage	Dist.	Elev.	Fac.	Landmark
591.5	11.5	1170'	Rd	Loomis-Oroville Road @ Nighthawk
593.0	1.5	1170'	C	Greater Columbia Water Trail Access Site #3
595.8	2.8	1107'	C	Palmer Lake Camp (parking lot)
599.8	4.0	1160'	W	Split Rock Picnic Area/Boat Ramp
602.0	2.2	1210'	Rd	Loomis-Oroville Road X Toats-Coulee Road
604.3	*2.3*	*1340'*	*R*	*Loomis (2.3 mi south of PNT) Post Office: 12 Palmer Ave. Loomis, WA 98827 509-223-4351 (Limited hours) Convenience store closed*
602.2	0.2	1180'	W	Sinlahekin Creek (Caution - fertilizer runoff)
603.4	1.2	1310'	TH	Toats-Coulee Road X Chopaka Grade Road – DNR Road 2200
606.7	3.3	3050'	Rd	Chopapka Grade Road - DNR Road 2200 X Lower Chopaka Grade Road
608.5	1.8	3080'	Rd	Chopaka Road X DNR Road 2420
609.1	*0.6*	*2950'*	*C*	*DNR Chopaka Lake Camp (0.6 mi north of PNT). No fee.*
609.0	0.5	3360'	TX	DNR Road 2420 X Old Jeep Road 392504H

Total Mileage	Dist.	Elev.	Fac.	Landmark
610.1	1.1	4070'	C	Old Jeep Road 392504H X Old Jeep Road 392505J @ Bear Pasture Cabin
610.6	0.5	4510'	W	Piped Spring
612.3	1.7	5490'	TX	Old Jeep Road 392505J X Ninemile Creek Road
612.9	0.6	5590'	W	Ninemile Creek Access
614.0	1.1	6080'	C-F	Cold Springs Camp (No fee)
614.2	0.2	6260'	C-F	Ninemile Creek Road @ Cold Springs Campground
615.1	0.9	5850'	W	Disappointment Creek
616.7	1.6	5800'	W	Swamp Creek
617.1	0.4	5730'	TX	Chopaka Mountain Trail X Forest Road E392404A
617.8	0.7	5760'	TX	Forest Road 392404A X Spur Trail to Goodenough Trail (Creek)
618.3	*0.5*	*5780'*	*C*	*Snowshoe Cabin (0.1 mi north of PNT)*
619.1	1.3	6870'	TX	Goodenough Trail @ Goodenough Park
619.6	0.5	6920'	TX	Goodenough Trail @ Pasayten Boundary
620.8	1.2	7120'	TX	Snowshoe Creek Trail 340 @ Zig-Zag Gate
622.7	1.9	7070'	W	Old site Lone Wolf Camp: Water but not a good campsite

Total Mileage	Dist.	Elev.	Fac.	Landmark
623.9	1.2	7010'	TX-C	Trail 340 X Trail 533 @ Horseshoe Pass with Trail Camp
624.1	0.2	6960'	W	Horseshoe Creek
624.8	0.7	7060'	C	Louden Lake
625.4	0.6	7000'	C	Coyote Camp (in old burn area)
626.7	1.3	6870'	W	Creek
627.4	0.7	6950'	C	Fireplace Camp
629.5	2.1	6980'	C	Dome Camp
630.8	1.3	6900'	TC	Boundary Trail 533 – Teapot Dome Camp
634.1	3.3	7110'	C	Trail Camp
634.9	0.8	6710'		Trail 533 @ Scheelite Pass
635.7	0.8	6660'	C	Creek
637.5	1.8	6720'		Trail 533 @ Old Tungsten Mine - Camp
638.1	0.6	6890'	C	Creek
642.3	4.2	7580'		Trail 533 @ Cathedral Pass
643.0	0.7	7410	C	Upper Cathedral Lakes Trail Camp
643.7	0.7	7260'	W	Creek
645.1	1.4	6940'	W	Creek under foot bridge
646.1	1.0	6740'	TX-C	Trail 533 X Andrews Creek Trail 504 @ Spanish Camp Patrol Cabin (Locked)
648.1	2.0	6960'	W	Creek - Water?
653.3	5.2	5090'	TX	Trail 533 X Ashnola River Trail 500
653.5	0.2	5100'	C	Ashnola Shelter
655.1	1.6	5900'	C	Trail Camp @ Park Pass Trail #506

Total Mileage	Dist.	Elev.	Fac.	Landmark
657.6	2.5	6910'	C	Trail 533 @ Barker Brown's Cabin - Trail Camp
658.7	1.1	6590'	W	Creek
659.7	1.0	6860'	TX	Trail 533 X Quartz Lake Spur Trail
660.2	*0.5*	*6770'*	*C*	*Quartz Lake Trail Camp (0.5 mi north of PNT)*
662.5	2.8	6350'	C	Dean Creek Trail Camp
665.4	2.9	7130'	TX	Trail 533 X Dean Creek Trail 456
665.9	0.5	6700'	C	Trail Camp
669.7	3.8	4220'	W	Creek
672.0	2.3	3910'	W	Trail 533 @ Pasayten River Crossing
672.2	*0.2*	*3930'*	*C*	*Pasayten Cabin (0.2 mi north of PNT)*
673.1	1.1	3960'	TX	Trail 533 X Robinson Creek Trail
675.5	2.4	4840'	*c*	Rainy Camp (abandoned)
676.7	1.2	5990'	TX	Trail 482 Monument 83 Trail
677.2	*0.5*	*6210'*	*W*	*Monument Spring (no reports - 0.5 north of PNT)*
678.9	2.2	4440'	W	Trail 533 @ Chuchuwanteen Creek
680.3	1.4	4600'	C	Trail Camp Spot
680.5	0.2	4600'	TX-C	Trail 533 X Trail 482 @ Chuchuwanteen Cabin - Trail Camp
684.1	3.6	5490'	W	Trail 533 @ Frosty Lake
685.9	1.8	6490'		Trail 533 @ Frosty Pass

Total Mileage	Dist.	Elev.	Fac.	Landmark
687.4	1.5	5520'	TX	Trail 533 X Pacific Crest National Scenic Trail 2000 (PCT 2646)
687.5	0.1	5580'	C	Trail Camp
689.7	2.2	6140'		PCT2000 @ Hopkins Pass
689.9	0.2	6180'	C	Spur Trail to Hopkins Lake Trail Camp
694.6	4.7	6660'	C	PCT2000 @ Woody Pass - Trail Camp (Caution: High Winds)
697.5	2.9	6220'	C	PCT2000 @ Trail Camp With Spring
699.7	2.2	5060'	TX	PCT2000 X Chancellor/Canyon Creek Trail 754 @ Holman Pass (PCT 2633)
700.4	0.7	4910'	C	Canyon Creek Trail Camp
701.5	1.1	5750'	C	Trail Camp
702.9	1.4	6300'	TX	Trail 754 X Devils Dome Trail 752 @ Sky Pilot Pass
706.4	3.5	5970'	C	Trail Camp past small stream
707.7	1.3	6130'	TX	Trail 752 X Jackita Ridge Trail 738 @ Devils Pass
712.0	4.3	6950'		Trail 752 @ Devils Dome
713.4	1.4	6090'	TX	Trail 752 @ Bear Skull Cabin
713.6	*0.2*	*6040'*	*C*	*Bear Skull Cabin (0.2 mi north of PNT)*

Total Mileage	Dist.	Elev.	Fac.	Landmark
718.4	5.0	1820'	TX	Trail 752 X Ross Lake East Bank Trail 736.
718.6	*0.2*	*1710'*	*C-P*	***RLNRA - Devil's Junction Camp (0.2 mi west of PNT) Permit from Wilderness Information Center in Marblemount, WA. (360) 854-7245***
718.6	*0.2*	*1800'*	*C-P*	***RLNRA - Devil's Creek Camp (0.2 mi north of PNT)***
722.0	3.6	1600'	C-P	RLNRA - Rainbow Point Camp
723.1	1.1	1770'	C-P	RLNRA - May Creek Camp
724.5	1.4	1920'	C-P	RLNRA - Roland Creek Camp
727.8	3.3	1930'	TX	Trail 736 X Jack Mountain Trail
728.3	*0.5*	*1910'*	*C-P*	***RLNRA - Hidden Hand Camp and Ruby Pasture Horse Camp***
730.2	2.4	1670'	W	Trail 736 @ Bridge Over Ruby Creek
735.0	4.8	1690'	Rd	Happy Panther Trail X Ross Lake Dam Service Road
736.0	1.0	1780'	W	Stream - good water
736.9	*0.9*	*1570'*	*R?*	***Ross Lake Resort - Mail Drop (0.3 mi east of PNT). 206.386.4437. Call in advance. Mail drop fee $20. Water taxi for fee to Trails on Ross Lake.***
741.4	5.4	1690'	C-P	RLNRA - Pumpkin Mountain Camp

Total Mileage	Dist.	Elev.	Fac.	Landmark
741.5	0.1	1610'	TX	West Bank Trail X Big Beaver Trail
741.8	*0.3*	*1670'*	*C-P*	*RLNRA - Big Beaver Camp (0.2 mi east of PNT)*
746.3	4.8	1780'	C-P	RLNRA - 39 mile Camp
747.9	1.6	1980'	C-P	Big Beaver Trail @ North Cascades National Park Boundary
750.1	2.2	2530'	C-P	NCNP - Luna Camp
754.3	4.2	3650'	C-P	Big Beaver Trail @ Beaver Pass Camp
754.5	0.2	3770'	C-P	NCNP - Beaver Pass Camp
757.4	2.7	2380'	W	Footbridge – Stream
757.7	0.3	2400	TX	Big Beaver Trail X Little Beaver Trail
758.7	1.0	2470'	C-P	NCNP - Stillwell Camp
761.2	2.5	2880'	C-P	NCNP - Twin Rocks Camp
763.3	2.1	3710"		Little Beaver Trail @ Climb to Whatcom Pass
764.3	1.0	5240'	TX	Little Beaver Trail X Brush Creek Trail @ Whatcom Pass
764.6	0.3	5010'	C-P	NCNP - Whatcom Camp
767.1	2.5	3130'	C-P	NCNP - Graybeal Camp
769.2	2.1	2790'	TX-C	Brush Creek Trail X Chilliwack Trail - Trail Camp
770.4	1.2	2540'	W	Chilliwack Trail @ Cable Car Crossing
771.1	0.7	2570'	C-P	NCNP - U.S. Cabin Camp
773.6	2.5	3220	C-P	NCNP - Cooper Creek Camp
776.0	2.4	4460'	TX-C	Chilliwack River Trail X Copper Ridge Trail and NCNP Boundary Camp

Total Mileage	Dist.	Elev.	Fac.	Landmark
777.2	1.2	5080'	TX-C	Chilliwack River Trail X Hannegan Pass Trail 674 (aka Ruth Creek Trail) and Hannegan Pass Trail Camp
781.2	4.0	3120'	Rd-C	Trail 674 X Ruth Creek Road (Road 32) - Hannegan Shelter Trail Camp
786.5	5.3	2030'	Rd	Road 32 X Mount Baker Highway (State Route 542)
799.7	*13.2*	*900'*	*R*	*Glacier, WA (13.2 mi west of PNT). No Post Office.*
786.7	0.2	2060'	C-F	NFS - Silver Fir Camp (Fee)
793.8	7.1	4140'	Rd	Mount Baker Highway @ Picture Lake
796.0	2.2	4760'	TX	Wild Goose Trail X Lake Ann Trail 600
798.4	2.4	3930'	TX	Lake Ann Trail 600 X Swift Creek Trail 607
801.4	3.0	3250'	W	Trail 607 @ Large Crevice and Stream
803.9	2.5	1620'	W	Swift Creek Trail 607 @ Swift Creek Ford
805.9	2.0	1360'	Rd	Swift Creek Trail 607 X Forest Road 1144
807.5	1.6	910'	C	Old Trail Camp ?
808.8	1.3	870'	Rd	Forest Road 1144 X Baker Lake Road (Road 11)
809.8	*1.0*	*730'*	*C-Fr*	*NFS - Panorama Point Camp (Fee) (1.0 mi south of waypoint). $16, res.*
809.3	*0.5*	*740'*	*C-Fr*	*NFS - Swift Creek Camp (0.5 mi southeast of PNT) $18, res.*
812.5	*3.7*	*790'*	*C-Fr*	*NFS - Shannon Creek Camp (0.3 mi south of PNT) $14, res.*

Total Mileage	Dist.	Elev.	Fac.	Landmark
814.7	5.9	740'	TH	Forest Road 11 X Baker Lake Trail 606
815.3	0.6	830'	TX	Trail 606 X East Bank Trail 610 (Baker Lake Trail 610) Bridge over Baker River
819.0	3.7	790'	C	Noisy Creek Camp
820.2	1.2	760'	C	Silver Creek Camp
824.4	4.2	720'	C	Maple Grove Camp
826.0	1.6	710'	C	Anderson Point Camp
827.2	1.4	970'	Rd	Trail 610 X Forest Road 1107
828.9	1.7	700'	C-F	NFS - Kulshan Camp (Fee)
830.1	1.2	850'	Rd	Forest Road 1106 X Baker Lake Road (Road 11)
841.1	*10.8*	*270'*	*R*	*Concrete, WA*
831.8	1.7	1550'	Rd	Forest Road 1114 X Forest Road 12
833.1	1.3	1910'	Rd	Forest Road 12 X Forest Road 13
835.2	2.1	2620'	Rd	Forest Road 13 X Old Forest Road
838.3	3.1	3370'	TH-W	Forest Road 13 X Park Butte Trail 603 (best water at TH creek)
839.4	1.1	3650'	W	Rocky Creek
840.4	1.0	4440'	TX	Trail 603 X Scott Paul Trail 603.1 (and hidden "stealth" trail camps)
840.7	0.4	4660'	TX	Trail 603 X Railroad Grade Trail 603.2
841.2	0.5	4850'	TX	Trail 603 X Bell Pass Trail 603.3

Total Mileage	Dist.	Elev.	Fac.	Landmark
842.2	*1.0*	*5400'*	*C*	*Park Butte Lookout (0.8 mi south of PNT) Great views of Mount Baker. (Water?)*
842.0	0.8	4420'	TX-C	Trail 603.3 X Ridley Creek Trail 696 and Mazama Park Trail Camp
844.5	2.5	4000'		Trail 603.3 @ Bell Pass
846.2	1.7	3110'	TX	Bell Pass Trail 603.3 X Forest Road 12
846.7	0.5	3200'	TX-C	Trail 603.3 X Elbow Lake Trail 697 and Creek
848.7	2.0	2090'	TX	Trail 607 X South Fork Nooksack Trail 602 @ Pioneer Horse Camp (a parking lot)
851.3	2.6	2040'	Rd	South Fork Nooksack Trail 602 X Forest Road 20
851.6	0.3	1900'	W	Wanlick Creek
852.3	0.7	1850'	Rd	Trail 602 X Mainline Road (Road 300)
853.3	1.0	2070'	Rd	Creek
854.9	1.6	1870'	W	Forest Road 300 X Forest Road 340
856.7	1.8	2840'	TH	Forest Road 340 X Huckleberry Trail
857.7	1.0	2820'	Rd	Huckleberry Trail X Forest Road 317
858.4	0.7	2980'	Rd	Forest Road 317 X Forest Road 310
860.6	2.2	2630'	Rd	Forest Road 310 X Forest Road 313

Total Mileage	Dist.	Elev.	Fac.	Landmark
862.0	1.4	3120'	TH	Forest Road 313 X East Josephine Ridge Trail
863.0	1.0	3957'	Rd	East Josephine Ridge Trail X Mount Josephine Truck Trail (MJTT)
864.9	1.9	2720'	Rd	Mount Josephine Truck Trail X Forest Road 310
869.0	4.1	1500'	Rd	Mount Josephine Truck Trail X Unnamed Forest Road
869.7	0.7	1160'	"TH"	Unnamed Forest Road X "Red Cabin Creek" Trail
870.4	0.7	510'	Rd	"Red Cabin Creek" Trail @ Crown Pacific Mainline Road
871.6	1.2	580'	Rd	Red Cabin Creek Trail X Crown Pacific Mainline Road
875.3	3.7	570'	Rd-C	Red Cabin Creek Trail X Scott Paper Road 110 - Trail Camp
879.7	4.4	2210'	Rd	Scott Paper Road 110 X Forest Road 130
880.4	0.7	2630'	W	Wiseman Creek
882.2	1.8	3510'	Rd	Forest Road 130 X Forest Road 150
882.7	0.5	3590'	Rd	Forest Road 150 X Forest Road 171
883.9	1.2	3650'	TH	Forest Road 171 X Gurdgieff Connector Trail (GCT)
885.6	1.7	4160'	TX	Gurdgieff Connector Trail @ Trail Split
893.4	7.8	480'	C	Quarry Trail Camp

Total Mileage	Dist.	Elev.	Fac.	Landmark
894.0	0.6	280'	Rd	Old Forest Road X Wickersham Road
895.5	1.5	300'	Rd	State Route 9 X Forest Road A-1900 Trouble with the landowner using this entrance. Recommend original route in another 1.7 miles south.
897.2	1.7	260'	Rd	*State Route 9 X Unnamed Forest Road. Preferred entrance to Anderson Mountain*
898.8	1.6	920'	W	Creek
901.6	2.8	2600'	Rd	Forest Road A-1900 X Anderson Mountain Shortcut
903.1	1.5	2690'	Rd	Forest Road A-1900 X Forest Road RD A-1000K
903.5	0.4	2820'	TH	Forest Road A-1000K X Anderson Mountain Trail
904.6	1.1	3210'	Rd	Anderson Mountain Trail X Forest Road A-1810
905.4	0.8	2990'	Rd	Forest Road A-1810 X Anderson Mountain Shortcut
906.9	1.5	2570'	C	Forest Road A-1810 X Unnamed Trail and Trail Camp (Water?)
907.8	0.9	1920'	TH-C	Unnamed Trail X Forest Road A-1600

Total Mileage	Dist.	Elev.	Fac.	Landmark
909.6	1.8	1050'	Rd	Unnamed Trail X Unnamed Forest Road (Jim Futrelle Trail?)
910.4	0.8	580'	Rd	Quarry Trail Camp (Water?)
910.6	0.2	470'	C	Unnamed Forest Road X Alger Creek CCC Road
912.3	1.7	300'	Rd	Cain Lake Road @ Trillium Gate
913.0	*0.7*	*260'*	*R*	*Alger, WA - Convenience Store (0.7 mi south of PNT)*
913.2	*0.9*	*280'*	*R*	*Alger, WA - Convenience Store/Bus Stop (0.9 mi west of PNT)*
913.8	1.5	910'	TH	Forest Road X South Ridge Trail
914.9	1.1	440'	W	Water Spigot
915.2	0.3	270'	Rd	Squires Lake Trail X Old Highway 99
917.3	2.1	510'	Rd	Summerland Road @ Bloedel Gate
919.5	2.2	1030'	Rd	Bloedel Forest Road X DNR Road B-100
920.0	0.5	1310'	TH	DNR Road 100 X British Army Trail (BAT)
920.9	0.9	1870'	C-PF	DNR - Lizard Lake
921.9	1.0	2000'	C-PF	DNR - Lily Lake
922.1	0.2	1990'	TH	DNR Tail X Max's Shortcut Trail
922.4	*0.3*	*1190'*	*C*	***Oyster Dome Trail Camp***
924.7	2.6	1260'	TH	Larry Reed Trail @ Blanchard Mountain Overlook

Total Mileage	Dist.	Elev.	Fac.	Landmark
925.1	0.4	1070'	TX	Larry Reed Trail X Oyster Dome Trail
926.6	1.5	110'	Rd	PNT X State Route 11
937.1	10.5	40'	Rd	Bay View-Edison Road @ Bay View State Park
940.9	3.8	10'	Rd	Whitney-Bay View Road X State Route 20
944.3	3.4	10'	Rd	State Route 20 X East March Point Road
949.1	4.8	20'	TH	March Point Road X Tommy Thompson Trail
951.8	2.7	30'	R	Tommy Thompson Trail X 22nd Street @ Anacortes Post Office: 519 Commercial Ave., Anacortes, WA 98221 360-299-6689
953.0	1.2	260'	TH	23rd Street X Trail 100 @ Anacortes Community Forest
955.5	2.5	340'	TX	Trail 241 X Havekost Road and Trail 224
957.7	2.2	420'	TX	Trail 25 X Trail 220 @ Anacortes
959.5	1.8	120'	TX	Lake Erie Store
959.6	0.1	110'	Rd	Heart Lake Road X Sharpe Road
960.1	0.5	90'	TH	Donnell Road X John Tursi Trail
962.7	2.6	130'	Rd	Bowman Hill Trail X Rosario Road
963.7	1.0	170'	TH	State Route 20 X Perimeter Trail @ Deception Pass Bridge

Total Mileage	Dist.	Elev.	Fac.	Landmark
965.5	*1.8*	*70'*	*C-F*	*Quarry Pond - Deception Pass State Park Satellite. (0.3 mi west of PNT off Cornet Bay Road). Hiker/biker site $12*
966.6	2.9	10'	TH	Comet Bay Road X Hoypus Point Trail @ Deception Pass State Park (Marina with showers)
969.0	2.4	110'	Rd	Hoypus Point Trail X Angler's Haven Drive
972.4	3.4	60'	Rd	North Jones Road X Dike Road
976.4	4.0	120'	R	State Route 20 X Ault Field Road - Oak Harbor, WA Post Office: 32199 WA-20, Oak Harbor, WA 98277 (360) 675-3000.
980.8	4.4	60'	TH - W	W. Crosby Road @ Whidbey State Park
987.0	6.2	5'	TH	Beach Trail @ Fort Ebey State Park
987.9	0.9	220'	C - Fr	Fort Ebey State Park Camp (Fee)
988.3	0.4	230'	W	Picnic Area: Water Spigot and Vault Toilets
991.0	2.7	20'	BW	Beach Walk @ Ebey's Landing
993.4	*2.4*	*120'*	*R*	*Coupeville, WA (2.4 mi east of PNT). Post Office: 201 NW Coveland St., Coupeville, WA 98239 360-678-5353*

Total Mileage	Dist.	Elev.	Fac.	Landmark
993.8	2.8	110'	W	Fort Casey State Park Picnic Area
994.5	0.7	10'	C-Fr	Fort Casey State Park Camp - RV/Tent $25 - very windy.
994.6	0.1	10'	F	State Route 20 @ Port Townsend-Keystone Ferry
1000.4	5.8	10'	R	Port Townsend Ferry Dock X Water Street
1001.4	1.0	10'	TH	Larry Scott Trail @ Port Townsend
1004.9	3.5	220'	Rd	Larry Scott Trail X Cape George Road
1008.9	4.0	130'	Rd	State Route 20 X Four Corners Road
1015.1	6.2	10'	Rd	State Route 20 X US Highway 101
1018.5	3.4	210'	Rd	US 101 X West Snow Creek Way
1021.6	3.1	720'	TH	Little Skidder Trail X Snow Creek Road – Road 2850
1023.9	2.3	1070'	Rd	Forest Road 2850 X Forest Road 2889
1026.7	2.8	2210'	BW-W	Forest Road 2889 X Bushwhack Point at Creek
1027.0	0.3	2380'	Rd	Bushwhack X Forest Road 2814
1028.5	1.5	3570'	TH	Snow Creek Trail 890 (estimated)
1030.3	1.8	4210'	TX	Trail 890 X Mount Zion Trail 836

Total Mileage	Dist.	Elev.	Fac.	Landmark
1032.0	1.7	2960'	TX	Trail 836 X Sleepy Hollow Trail 852 @ Gold Creek Road - Road 28
1034.1	2.1	2230'	Rd	Trail 852 X Old Forest Road 2830.
1034.8	0.7	2100'	W	Gold Creek
1036.6	1.8	2680'	Rd	Trail 852 X Old Forest Road 030
1038.3	1.7	2670'	W	Creek
1039.9	1.6	2620'	TX	Trail 852 X Gold Creek Trail 830
1040.1	0.2	2660'	W	Creek (Water?)
1043.1	3.0	3260'	TH	Forest Road 2870 X Tubal Cain Trail 840
1043.2	0.1	3280'	C	Silver Creek Shelter Trail Camp
1046.6	3.4	4320'	C	Tubal Cain Trail 840 @ Copper Creek and Trail camp
1048.6	2.0	5200'	TX	Trail 840 X Spur Trail to Buckhorn Lake
1048.9	*0.3*	*5150'*	*C*	***Buckhorn Lake Camp (0.3 mi east of PNT)***
1051.6	3.0	5980'	TX	Trail 840 X Upper Dungeness Trail 833.2 X Upper Big Quilcene Trail 833.1 @ Marmot Pass
1053.3	1.7	4920'	TX-C	Trail 833.2 X Home Lake Trail 893 @ Boulder Shelter
1056.6	3.3	5340'	C-P	ONP - Home Lake Camp. Permit. No fires.

Total Mileage	Dist.	Elev.	Fac.	Landmark
1057.0	0.4	5840'	TX	Trail 893 X Constance Pass Trail (CPT)
1058.9	1.9	5040'	C-P	ONP - Sunnybrook Meadows Camp
1061.8	2.9	2190'	TX	Constance Pass Trail X Dosewallips River Trail (DRT) (estimated)
1062.9	*1.1*	*1860'*	*C-P*	***ONP - Dose Forks Camp (1.1 mi east of PNT). Permit.***
1064.9	3.1	2640'	W	Dosewallips River Trail @ Burdick Creek
1066.7	1.8	3170'	C-P	ONP - Deception Creek Camp. Permit.
1067.3	0.6	3280'	C-P	ONP - Camp Marion (unofficial)
1069.7	2.4	3870'	C-P	Dosewallips River Trail @ ONP - Bear Camp. Permit. No fires.
1071.4	1.7	4470'	TH-C-Pr	Dosewallips River Trail X Lost Pass Trail @ ONP - Dose Meadows Camp. Permit.
1073.5	2.1	5850'	TX	Dosewallips River Trail X Hayden Pass Trail (HPT) @ Hayden Pass
1081.8	8.3	1800'	TX	Hayden Pass Trail X Elwha River Trail (ERT) at ONP - Hayes River Camp & Ranger Station
1082.1	0.3	1650'	C-P	ONP - Chateau Camp. Permit.
1082.7	0.6	1600'	C-P	ONP - Tipperary Shelter Camp. Permit.
1086.6	3.9	1410'	C-P	ONP - Stoney Point Camp. Permit.

Total Mileage	Dist.	Elev.	Fac.	Landmark
1086.7	0.1	1420'	C-P	Elwha River Trail @ ONP - Elkhorn Camp & Ranger Station. Permit.
1087.8	1.1	1370'	C-P	ONP - Canyon Camp. Permit.
1089.3	1.5	1250	C-P	ONP - Mary's Falls Camp. Permit.
1092.9	3.6	1370'	C-P	Elwha River Trail @ ONP - Lillian Camp (Footbridge)
1094.9	2.0	1120'		Elwha River Trail @ Michael's Ranch
1095.5	*0.6*	*810'*	*C-P*	*Humes Ranch Camp (0.6 mi southeast of PNT)*
1096.8	1.9	1160'	C-P	Elwha River Trail X Whiskey Bend Road and ONP - Whiskey Bend Horse Camp
1100.8	4.0	370'	Rd	Whiskey Bend Road X Olympic Hot Springs Road and Ranger Station
1101.7	*0.9*	*310'*	*C-F*	*ONP - Elwha Camp (0.9 mi north of PNT). 2016 - Flood destroyed.*
1108.8	*8.0*	*230'*	*R*	*Port Angeles, WA (8.0 mi northeast of the PNT). Post Office: 424 E. 1st St., Port Angeles, WA 98362 360-417-7528*
1101.5	0.7	500'	C-F	ONP - Altair Camp. 2016 - Flood destroyed.
1104.8	3.3	1520'	Rd	Olympic Hot Springs Road @ Overlook

Total Mileage	Dist.	Elev.	Fac.	Landmark
1109.0	4.2	2150'	TX	Olympic Hot Springs Trail @ ONP -Boulder Creek Camp, Olympic Hot Springs
1114.4	*5.4*	*5180'*	*C-P*	*ONP - Appleton Pass Camp (0.3 mi south of trail). Permit. No fires.*
1114.2	5.2	5050'		Appleton Pass Trail @ Appleton Pass
1116.5	2.3	3090'	TX CP	Appleton Pass Trail X Sol Duc River Trail and ONP - Appleton Junction Camp. Limited permits, Res.
1116.9	0.4	3150	C-Pr	ONP - Rocky Creek Camp. Limited permits, Res.
1117.1	0.2	3250'	C-Pr	ONP - Upper Sol Duc Bridge. Limited permits, Res.
1118.6	1.5	4220'	C-Pr	Sol Duc River Trail @ ONP - Sol Duc Park Camp & Ranger Station. Permit. Res. No fires.
1119.4	0.8	4780'	C-Pr	ONP - Heart Lake Camp. Permit. Res. No fires.
1119.6	0.2	4830'	TX	Sol Duc River Trail X High Divide Trail (HDT)
1122.8	*3.2*	*4520'*	*C-Pr*	*ONP - Hoh Lake Camp (1.1 mi south of PNT). Permit. Res. No fires.*
1121.7	2.1	4910'	TX	High Divide Trail @ Seven Lakes Spur Trail

Total Mileage	Dist.	Elev.	Fac.	Landmark
1122.3	*0.6*	*4500'*	*C-Pr*	***ONP - Lunch Lake Camp (0.6 mi north of PNT). Permit. Res. No fires.***
1124.9	3.2	3550'	C-Pr	High Divide Trail X Low Divide/Deer Lake Cutoff Trail at ONP - Deer Lake Camp
1128.5	3.6	4080'	TX	Low Divide Trail X Bogachiel River Trail (BRT)
1132.4	3.9	2210'	C-P	Bogachiel River Trail @ ONP -Twenty-One Mile Camp. (Unofficial)
1135.3	2.9	1490'	C-P	ONP - Hyak Shelter. Permit.
1138.4	3.1	1040'	C-P	Bogachiel River Trail @ ONP - Fifteen Mile Shelter. Permit.
1142.2	3.8	670'	C-P	ONP - Flapjack Camp. Permit.
1145.9	3.7	450'	TX CP	Bogachiel River Trail X Indian Pass Trail and ONP - Bogachiel Camp. Permit.
1149.9	4.0	360'		Bogachiel River Trail @ Exit Olympic National Park
1151.4	1.5	490'	Rd	Bogachiel River Trail X North Bogachiel Road - Road 2932
1156.6	5.2	240'	C-F	North Bogachiel Road X US Highway 101 @ Bogachiel State Park

Total Mileage	Dist.	Elev.	Fac.	Landmark
1162.0	**5.4**	**300'**	***R***	***Forks, WA (5.4 miles north of PNT). Post Office: 61 S, Spartan Ave. Forks, WA 98331 360-374-6303***
1161.1	4.5	800'	Rd	Road G2000 X Forest Road G2500
1165.2	4.1	120'	Rd	Road G2500 Forest Road G3000
1165.3	0.2	540'	Rd-W	Road G3000 X Forest Road RY3300 and Goodman Creek
1166.9	1.6	540'	Rd	Road G3000 X Forest Road RY3300
1168.3	1.4	290'	Rd	Road G3000 X Forest Road RY3400
1168.9	0.6	330'	W	Creek (Water?)
1173.6	4.7	400'	Rd	Road G3000 X Oil City Road
1176.5	2.9	50'	W	Hoh River Access
1178.8	2.3	40'	TH	Oil City Road End @ Olympic National Park
1180.7	1.9	30'	BW CP	Beach Walk @ Hoh Head Trail @ Ladders and Bluff Trail Camp. Permit. Bear Canister.
1183.9	3.2	70'	C-P	Hoh Head Trail @ ONP - Mosquito Creek Camp. Permit. Bear Canister.
1185.4	1.5	20'	TH	Beach Walk @ Alternate Goodman Creek Bypass
1188.3	2.9	15'	BW	Beach Walk @ ONP - Toleak Point Camp. Permit. Bear Canister.

Total Mileage	Dist.	Elev.	Fac.	Landmark
1189.6	1.3	30'	C-P	ONP - Strawberry Point Camp. Permit. Bear Canister.
1190.7	1.1	10'	BW CP	Beach Walk @ ONP - Scotts Creek Camp. Permit. Bear Canister.
1193.2	2.5	10'	TH C-P	Beach Walk X Third Beach Trail and ONP - Third Beach Camp. Permit. Bear Canister.
1194.6	1.4	270'	RD	Third Beach Trail X La Push Road
1195.9	*1.3*	*20'*	*C-P*	***ONP - Second Beach Camp (0.8 mi west of PNT). Permit. Bear Canister.***
1196.6	2.0	20'	R	Lonesome Creek General Store & Post Office: 500 Ocean Dr., La Push, WA 98350 360-374-5378 (Limited hours)
1197.1	0.5	20'		Center of La Push @ Quillayute River
1199.5	2.4	30'	C-P	ONP - Hole-in-the-Wall Camp. Permit. Bear Canister.
1200.9	1.4	20'	BW C-P	Beach Walk @ ONP - Chilean Memorial Camp. Permit. Bear Canister.
1205.7	4.8	20'	BW C-P	Beach Walk @ ONP - Cedar Creek Camp. Permit. Bear Canister.

Total Mileage	Dist.	Elev.	Fac.	Landmark
1207.1	1.4	10'	BW C-P	ONP - Norwegian Memorial Camp and Ranger Patrol Station. Permit. Bear Canister.
1211.2	4.1	20'	BW C-Pr	Beach Walk @ ONP - Yellow Banks Camp. Permit. Bear Canister. Res.
1213.0	1.8	10'	BW C-Pr	ONP - South Sand Point Camp. Permit. Bear Canister. Res., No fires.
1213.8	0.8	20'	BW C-Pr	ONP - Sand Point Camp and Ranger Patrol Station. Permit. Bear Canister. Res., No fires.
1215.8	2.0	20'	BW C-Pr	Beach Walk @ ONP - Wedding Rock Camp. Permit. Bear Canister. Res., No fires.
1217.0	1.2	20'	TH C-Pr	Beach Walk @ ONP - Cape Alava Camp and Trail. Permit. Bear Canister. Res., No fires.
1220.2	3.2	60'	C-F	*ONP - Ozette Camp (3.6 mi east of PNT). $15*
1220.7	3.7	90'	C-R	*Lost Resort, Ozette, WA (Limited Food - 3.7 mi east of PNT). $15 tent site.*

TRAIL ALTERNATE ROUTES

MONTANA

The Original PNT Northern Route to Kintla Lakes and Beyond

Total Mileage	Dist.	Elev.	Fac.	Landmark
34.4	0.0	6270'	TX	Boulder Pass Trail X Bowman Lake Trail
36.0	1.6	6590'	TX	BPT X Hole-in-the-Wall Camp Trail
36.7	*0.7*	*6340'*	*C-PFr*	*GNP - Hole-in-the Wall Camp (0.7 mi west pf Alt PNT). Permit. $5 fee. Res. after 8/1.*
39.1	3.1	7210'	C-PFr	GNP - Boulder Pass Camp. Permit. $5 fee. Res. after 8/1.
44.6	5.5	4380'	C-PFr	Boulder Pass Trail @ GNP - Upper Kintla Lake Camp
49.7	5.1	4020'	C-PFr	GNP - Kintla Lake Head Camp. Permit. $5 fee. Res. after 6/15.
52.0	2.3	4190'	TX	Boulder Pass Trail X Kintla-Starvation Ridge Trail
55.6	3.6	4020'	C-F	GNP - Kintla Lake Camp. Car/tent camp. $15
56.0	0.4	4070'	Rd	Boulder Pass Trail X Kintla Lake Road
57.5	1.5	3990'	TH	Kintla Lake Road X Kishenehn Trail

Total Mileage	Dist.	Elev.	Fac.	Landmark
61.7	4.2	3880'	TX-W	Kishenehn Trail X Kintla Creek Trail and Creek
62.4	0.7	3880'	C-W	Fording North Fork Flathead River and Trail Camp
64.8	2.4	3980'	Rd	Private Road X North Fork Road 486
68.4	3.6	4210'	TH	Trail Creek Road X Thoma Trail 15 (New Trailhead)
68.8	*0.4*	*4240'*	*W*	*Piped Spring (0.4 mi west of Alt PNT)*
72.2	3.8	7104'		Trail 15 @ Thoma Lookout
74.0	1.8	7010'	TX	Trail 15 X Thoma-Colts Creek Trail 18
75.0	1.0	6170'	W	Creek Crossing (Water?)
76.0	1.0	5400'	Rd	Trail 18 X Forest Road 114A and Creek Crossing
76.8	0.8	5100'	TH	Forest Road 114A X Thoma-Tuchuck Trail 19
80.9	4.1	7260'	TX	Trail 19 X Tuchuck Ridge Trail 114
83.2	2.3	7745'		Trail 19 @ Tuchuck Mountain – Highest Point on the PNT
83.7	0.5	7216'	BW	Bushwhack @ 7216' Peak
84.5	0.8	7125'	BW	Bushwhack @ 7125' Peak
85.9	1.4	5270'	Rd	Bushwhack X Frozen Lake Road - RD114Y

Total Mileage	Dist.	Elev.	Fac.	Landmark
87.2	*1.3*	*5000'*	*C*	*Weasel Cabin (0.2 mi east of Alt PNT)*
88.1	2.2	5120'	Rd	Forest Road 414Y X Forest Road 319
90.3	2.2	5750'	W	Camp Creek
94.6	4.3	6390'	TX	Trail 77 X Highline Trail 339

The Original PNT to Ten Lakes Scenic Area

Total Mileage	Dist.	Elev.	Fac.	Landmark
105.4	0.0	6220'	TX	Trail 339 X Clarence-Rich Creek Trail 78
106.4	1.0	5430'	W	Rich Creek
108.2	1.8	4950'	Rd	Trail 78 X Forest Road 7103
108.5	0.3	4900'	W	Bridge - Rich Creek
109.7	1.2	4990'	Rd	Forest Road 7103 X Forest Road 7086
110.2	0.5	4930	C	Wigwam River - Trail Camp
112.3	2.1	5550'	Rd	Forest Road 7086 X Forest Road 7091
114.1	1.8	5990'	TH	Forest Road 7091 X Rainbow Trail 89
118.6	4.5	7490'	TX	Trail 86 X Highline Trail 339
119.7	1.1	7270'	TX	Trail 339 X Blacktail Trail 92. Re-join Primary PNT.

The Original PNT Northern Route to Northwest Peak

Total Mileage	Dist.	Elev.	Fac.	Landmark
203.7	0.0	4660'	Rd	Forest Road 338 X Forest Road 5902
204.3	0.6	4610'	W	Yaak River
206.2	1.9	5680'	W	Winkum Creek
210.1	3.9	6210'	TH	Forest Road 338 X New Northwest Peak Trail 169
213.0	2.9	7709'		Trail 169 @ Northwest Peak
213.4	0.4	7360'	BW	Bushwhack Point on Northwest Peak
214.9	1.5	7583'	BW	Bushwhack @ Davis Mountain
216.9	2.0	6390'	TX	Trail 174 X Trail 164 Re-join primary PNT

Alternate Route: Long Canyon Creek Trail 16 to Bypass the Burn Area on Parker Ridge

Total Mileage	Dist.	Elev.	Fac.	Landmark
255.1	0.0	1900'	TH-C	Road 18 X Trail 14 / Parker Ridge Trail 221 - Parker Creek Trail Camp (Must Fill Water!)
258.6	3.5	1860'	TH	Long Canyon Creek #16 Trailhead (estimate)
260.6	2.0	2580'		Curve into the Canyon Creek drainage (estimate)

Total Mileage	Dist.	Elev.	Fac.	Landmark
262.1	1.5	3040'		Trail begins decent into canyon (estimate)
263.8	1.7	3760'	TX	Trail junction with unmaintained TR424 (estimate)
265.6	1.8	3950'		Walkways lead to the first crossing of Canyon Creek (estimate)
272.6	7.0	4540'	TX	Long Canyon Creek Trail 7 - climb to PNT (estimate)
274.4	1.8	6400'	TX	Trail 221 X Pyramid Pass Trail 13

IDAHO – WASHINGTON

Hughes Meadow to Sullivan Lake

Total Mileage	Dist.	Elev.	Fac.	Landmark
309.8	0.0	2950'	TX	Trail 312 X Trail 311
314.6	4.8	5530'	TX	Trail 311 X Trail 512
319.5	4.9	6030'	TX	Trail 512 X Gold Creek Trail 320 (Abandoned)
321.2	1.7	5440'	TX	Trail 512 X Forest Road 302
321.6	0.4	5390'	TH-W	Forest Road 302 X Grassy Mtn NRT Trail 503
324.1	2.5	6180'	TH	Trail 503 X Hall Mtn Trail 533
328.8	4.7	5560'	TX	Trail 533 X Noisey Creek Trail 588
333.8	5.0	2620'	Rd	Trail 588 X Noisy Creek Campground

Total Mileage	Dist.	Elev.	Fac.	Landmark
334.3	0.5	2630'	TH	Campground Roads X Lake Shore Trail 504
339.0	4.7	2560'	Rd	Forest Road 22 X Sullivan Lake Road

WASHINGTON

Circumnavigating the Leola Creek Bushwhack

Total Mileage	Dist.	Elev.	Fac.	Landmark
324.0	0.0	4340'	Rd	Trail 511 X Forest Road 2220
324.5	0.5	4190'	C	Gypsy Meadows Trail Camp
327.2	2.7	3640'	Rd	Easy Access to Sullivan Creek
329.0	1.8	3290'	Rd	Forest Road 2220 X Sullivan Creek Road - RD22
331.2	2.2	3290'	Rd	Forest Road 22 X Forest Road 300
336.5	*5.3*	*2630'*	*C-Fr*	*NFS - East Sullivan Lake Camp (0.5 mi south of Alt PNT). $16, Res.*
336.7	5.5	2560'	Rd	Forest Road 22 X Sullivan Lake Road
336.9	*0.2*	*2610'*	*Rgr*	*NFS Sullivan Lake Ranger Station (0.2 mi south of Alt PNT)*
340.6	3.9	2530'	Rd	Sullivan Lake Road X Lime Lake Road
343.6	3.0	2090'	R	State Route 31 @ Metaline Falls, Washington. Re-join primary PNT.

Original PNT Route Across Boundary Dam

Total Mileage	Dist.	Elev.	Fac.	Landmark
338.3	0.0	3620'	TH	Trail 507 X Halliday Trail 522
341.0	2.7	3000'	C	Trail Camp
342.2	1.2	2520'	Rd	Trail 522 X State Route 31
347.3	5.1	2520'	Rd	State Route 31 X East Side Road – RD3165
347.7	0.4	2650'	C	NFS - Crescent Lake Camp (no fee - disgusting camp)
349.4	1.7	2260'	W	East Side Road @ Boundary Dam Visitor Center with water spigot, flush toilets, power.
350.1	0.7	2000'	Rd	Boundary Dam Access Road West of the Dam
350.2	0.1	2010'	C	Boundary Dam Campground (No Fee)
356.8	6.6	2580'	Rd	Boundary Road X Flume Creek Road – RD350

Kettle Crest North - Wildfire Closure Alternate Route

Total Mileage	Dist.	Elev.	Fac.	Landmark
416.3	0.0	1470'	Rd	Sand Creek Road – RD4013 X Rock Cut Road - RD4141
420.2	3.9	1440'	R	Town of Orient. Post Office: 365 Main St , Orient, WA 99160 (509) 684-5886
422.8	2.6	1450'	Rd	US395 X Boulder Creek Road
424.7	1.9	1960'	Rd	Boulder Creek Rd X FR6110
426.8	2.1	2280'	Rd	FR6110 X FR105
427.5	0.7	2370'	W	FR6110 X Tom Creek
429.3	1.8	2550'	W	FR6110 X Echo Creek
429.7	0.4	2580'	C	FR6110 @ Slide Creek Trail Camp
435.0	5.3	3490'	Rd	FR6110 X FR6113
436.4	1.4	3800'	Rd	South Boulder Creek Rd - FR6110 X Indian Creek Rd - FR430 Approx. east boundary of Kettle Crest wildfire burn area
437.7	1.3	4040'	Rd	South Boulder Creek RD - FR6110 (FR2030) X FR6114
437.8	0.1	4060'	C	Trail Camp
438.6	0.8	4230'	Rd	FR2030 X FR900
443.3	4.7	5480'	TH	FR2030 X Old Stage TR75
445.3	2.0	6070'	TX	Trail 13 X Old Stage Road Trails 1 / 75. Re-join PNT

Edds Mountain Trail 3 to Thirteenmile Trail 23

Total Mileage	Dist.	Elev.	Fac.	Landmark
467.5	0.0	6110'	BW	Trail 3 @ Bushwhack Point
469.2	1.7	4890'	BW	Trail 3 @ Alternate Bushwhack Point
469.8	0.6	4300'	BW	Bushwhack X Old Forest Road 630
470.5	0.7	3920'	Rd	Forest Road 630 X Forest Road 600
472.5	2.0	4590'	Rd	PNT Rejoin on Hall Creek Road - Forest Road 600. Re-join PNT.

Original PNT Stock Route – Thirteenmile Trail #23

Total Mileage	Dist.	Elev.	Fac.	Landmark
481.3	0.0	3690'	Rd	Trail 23 X Bushwhack Point.
483.2	1.9	3020'	BW	Creek
484.7	1.5	2010'	W	Trail 23 X State Route 21 and NFS Thirteenmile Camp
487.0	2.3	2110'	Rd-C	Bushwhack X State Route 21. Re-join primary PNT.

Forest Road 100 to Swan Lake and to Forest Road 500

Total Mileage	Dist.	Elev.	Fac.	Landmark
488.6	0.0	3360'	Rd	Trail 25 X Forest Road 100.
491.3	2.7	3170'	Rd	Forest Road 100 X Scatter Creek Road – RD53 and Creek
492.2	0.9	3330'	Rd	Forest Road 53 X Forest Road 500
493.3	1.1	3640'	Rd	Forest Road 53 X Forest Road 500
493.9	*0.6*	*3690'*	*C-F*	*NFS - Swan Lake Camp (Fee) (0.6 mi north of Alt PNT). Likely closed due to 2015 wildfires. Lake access should be open.*
494.5	1.2	3630'	W	Spring (cow trashed)
498.6	4.1	3770'	Rd	Forest Road 5314 X Forest Road 500. Re-join primary PNT route.

New Alternate: Corner Butte-Sweat Creek Trail 301 South

Total Mileage	Dist.	Elev.	Fac.	Landmark
504.7	0.0	4190'	Rd	Forest Road 3125 X Forest Road 31
505.2	0.5	4260'	TH	Forest Road 32 @ New Trailhead
506.5	1.3	4330'		New Trail X Forest Road 035
508.9	2.4	4370'		New Trail X Forest Road 030
509.3	0.4	4170'		New Trail X Forest Road 020

Total Mileage	Dist.	Elev.	Fac.	Landmark
510.4	1.1	3460'	Rd-W	Forest Road 31 @ Granite Creek
510.9	0.5	3520'	Rd-C	Forest Road 31 X State Route 20 and Stealth Trail Camp

Original PNT Route to Climb Bonaparte Mountain

Total Mileage	Dist.	Elev.	Fac.	Landmark
535.8	0.0	5830'	TX	Trail 308 X Fourth of July Trail 307
536.9	1.1	5760'	TX	Trail 308 X Bonaparte Trail 306
537.0	0.1	5780'	W	Lookout Spring - Good Water
538.1	1.1	6910'	TX	Trail 306 X Antoine Trail 304
538.6	*0.5*	*7260'*	*C*	*Mount Bonaparte Summit Trail Camp (No Water - 0.5 mi south of Alt PNT)*
541.0	2.9	5040'	W	Antoine Creek East
541.4	0.4	4880'	TX	Trail 307 X Antoine Trail 304
535.8	0.0	5830'	TX	Trail 308 X Fourth of July Trail 307

Original PNT Route Harrison Camp Trail 478 / Trail 453

Total Mileage	Dist.	Elev.	Fac.	Landmark
673.1	0.0	3960'	TX	Trail 533 X Robinson Creek Trail 478.
677.7	4.6	4280'	TX	Trail 478 X Trail 453 @ Pasayten Airfield
681.2	3.5	4600'	C	Trail 533 X Trail 478 @ Chuchuwanteen Cabin - Trail Camp

Original PNT Route Ross Lake North to Little Beaver Creek Trail and Into North Cascades National Park

Total Mileage	Dist.	Elev.	Fac.	Landmark
718.4	0.0	1820'	TX	Trail 752 X Ross Lake East Bank Trail 736.
718.6	0.2	1800'	C-P	RLNRA - Devil's Creek Camp
720.8	*2.2*	*1620'*	*C-P*	*RLNRA - Dry Creek Camp (0.2 mi south of Alt PNT - Lake levels may be an island). Permit.*
722.2	3.6	1630'	C-P	Trail 736 @ RLNRA - Lightening Creek Camp
726.2	4.0	1610'	C-P	Boat Ride to RLNRA – Little Beaver Creek Camp
729.1	2.9	2060'		Little Beaver Creek Trail @ North Cascades National Park Boundary
735.8	6.7	2400'	TX	Big Beaver Trail X Little Beaver Trail

Baker Lake to Mount Josephine

Total Mileage	Dist.	Elev.	Fac.	Landmark
805.9	0.0	1360'	Rd	Swift Creek Trail 607 X Forest Road 1144
806.7	0.8	1630'	Rd	Forest Road 1144 X Forest Road 1130
807.1	0.4	1570'	W	Morovitz Creek
808.5	1.4	1170'	W	Park Creek
809.9	1.4	1040'	Rd	Forest Road 1130 X Baker Lake Road
810.0	0.1	1030'	C-F	NFS - Boulder Cr Camp
813.8	3.8	740'	Rd	Baker Lake Road X Forest Road 1114
817.7	3.9	940'	W	Bear Creek
823.4	5.7	830'	Rd	Baker Lake Road X Forest Road 310 at Grandy Lake County Park
825.0	1.6	1570'	W	Bridge - Grandy Creek
826.6	1.6	2450'	Rd	Forest Road 310 @ Gate
827.3	0.7	2830'	W	Road Washout - Creek (Water?)
829.6	2.3	2980'	Rd	Forest Road 317 X Forest Road 310

Mount Josephine – Les Hilde Trail

Total Mileage	Dist.	Elev.	Fac.	Landmark
860.6	0.0	2630'	Rd	Forest Road 310 X Forest Road 313
861.1	0.5	2870'	TH	Forest Road 313 X Les Hilde Trail
862.9	1.8	1790'	TH	Forest Road 2000 X Lower Josephine Lake Trail.
864.8	1.9	990'	Rd	Les Hilde Trail X Forest Road 2000
865.5	0.7	1160'	TH	Unnamed Forest Road X "Red Cabin Creek" Trail

Anacortes Bypass

Total Mileage	Dist.	Elev.	Fac.	Landmark
944.3	0.0	10'	Rd	State Route 20 X East March Point Road
947.3	3.0	10'	TH	Christensen Road X Saterlee Road @ Similk Beach
950.8	3.5	110'	TH	Heart Lake Road X Sharpe Road. Re-join primary PNT.

Original PNT Route West at Deception Pass

Total Mileage	Dist.	Elev.	Fac.	Landmark
963.7	0.0	170'	TH	State Route 20 X Perimeter Trail @ Deception Pass Bridge
964.6	0.9	10'	C-Fr	Deception Pass State Park Camp $30, res.
966.8	2.2	10'	Rd	Beach Walk @ West Powell Road
967.6	0.8	110'	Rd	Banta Road X State Route 20
973.0	5.4	120'	Rd	State Route 20 X Ault Field Road. Re-join primary PNT.

Visit Oak Harbor and Rejoin PNT at Whidbey State Park

Total Mileage	Dist.	Elev.	Fac.	Landmark
976.4	0.0	120'	R	State Route 20 X Ault Field Road
981.9	5.5	60'	Rd	W. Crosby Road @ Whidbey State Park

Original PNT Route Uncas Road - Hurricane Hill Trail

Total Mileage	Dist.	Elev.	Fac.	Landmark
1015.1	0.0	10'	Rd	State Route 20 X US Highway 101
1016.2	1.1	70'	Rd	West Uncas Road X Salmon Creek Road – Road 2986
1017.4	1.2	470'	Rd	Forest Road 2986 X Unnamed Forest Road

Total Mileage	Dist.	Elev.	Fac.	Landmark
1018.4	1.0	500'	Rd	Forest Road 2986 X Old Forest Road
1020.3	1.9	980'	Rd	Forest Road 2986 X Snow Creek Road – Road 2850
1021.6	1.3	770'	W	Snow Creek Access
1022.4	0.8	620'	Rd	Forest Road 2850 X Jimmycomelately Road – Road 2855
1023.7	1.3	910'	W	Jimmycomelately Creek
1026.5	2.8	1400'	Rd	Forest Road 2855 X Palo Alto Road
1028.1	1.6	1360'	Rd	Palo Alto Road X Junction Forest Road 2880 and 310
1029.2	1.1	870'	C-F	NFS - Dungenesse Forks Camp. $14
1030.0	0.8	960'	TH	Forest Road 2927 X Gray Wolf Trail 834
1031.1	1.1	1430'	Rd	Old Forest Road 2880 X Forest Road 2870
1035.6	4.5	1390'	Rd	Old Forest Road 2880 X Forest Road 2875
1039.1	3.5	2550'	TH	Trail 838 X Deer Ridge Trail 846
1044.1	5.0	5230'	TH – C- Pr	Trail 846 @ Deer Park Camp, Olympic National Park
1048.4	4.3	6030'	C-Pr	ONP - Roaring Winds Camp (No Water)
1049.5	1.1	6620'	TX	Trail 836 X Badger Valley Trail
1051.6	2.1	6130'	TX	Trail 836 X Obstruction Point, Olympic Nat Park

Total Mileage	Dist.	Elev.	Fac.	Landmark
1059.3	7.7	5250'	Rd	Obstruction Peak Road @ Hurricane Ridge Visitors Center
1060.6	1.3	5090'	TH	Heart of the Hills Road X Hurricane Hill Trail (HHT)
1066.4	5.8	370'	Rd	Whiskey Bend Road X Olympic Hot Springs Road. Re-join primary PNT.

Olympic National Forest Connecter Route

Total Mileage	Dist.	Elev.	Fac.	Landmark
1028.1	0.0	1360'	Rd	Palo Alto Road X Junction Forest Road 2880 and 310
1028.8	0.7	1620'	Rd	Forest Road 28 X Old Forest Road 2880
1030.2	1.4	1250'	W	Eddy Creek
1031.7	1.5	1200'	TH	Old Forest Road 2880 X Gold Creek Trail at Gold Creek Bridge
1031.9	0.2	1260'	C	Old Gold Creek Shelter - Possible Trail Camp?
1034.2	2.3	2620'	TX	Trail 852 X Gold Creek Trail 830.

Grand Pass Detour Route

Total Mileage	Dist.	Elev.	Fac.	Landmark
1071.2	0.0	4470'	TH – C- Pr	Dosewallips River Trail X Lost Pass Trail @ ONP - Dose Meadows Camp. Permit.
1075.1	3.9	4940'	C	Forest Road 28 X Old Forest Road 2880
1076.6	1.5	4180'	TX	Lost Pass Trail @ Upper Cameron Basin Camp
1079.7	3.1	5410'	TX	Lost Pass Trail X Grand Pass Trail X Cameron Creek Trail
1077.2	0.6	5060'	C	Grand Pass Trail @ Moose Lake Camp. Privy
1080.2	0.5	4940'	C	Grand Pass Train X Grand Valley Trail X Badger Valley Trail
1084.0	3.8	6130'	TH	Grand Valley Trail @ Obstruction Point

Goodman Creek Shortcut to Pacific Ocean Bypassing Oil City

Total Mileage	Dist.	Elev.	Fac.	Landmark
1165.3		540'	Rd-W	Road G3000 X Forest Road RY3300
1166.0	0.7	300'	W	Branch Goodman Creek
1166.4	0.4	540'	Rd-W	Forest Road RY3310 X Unnamed Forest Road
1166.9	0.5	500'	TH	Forest Road X Unnamed Trail
1167.6	0.7	20'	BW	Beach Walk @ Alternate Goodman Creek Bypass

SUPPORT THE
PACIFIC NORTHWEST NATIONAL
SCENIC TRAIL

If you would like to support the trail, or need more information, please contact:

Pacific Northwest Trail Association

http://www.pnt.org

info@pnt.or**g**

1851 Charles Jones Memorial Circle #4
Sedro-Woolley, WA 98285
Phone: (360) 854-9415

For a complete description of the trail and all the alternate routes, look for --

Search for it at: Amazon.com

You're off to great places!
Today is your day!
Your MOUNTAIN is waiting
so get on your WAY!

Dr. Seuss

70814737R00044

Made in the USA
Middletown, DE
17 April 2018